First World War
and Army of Occupation
War Diary
France, Belgium and Germany

15 DIVISION
Headquarters, Branches and Services
General Staff
1 September 1916 - 30 September 1916

WO95/1913/1

The Naval & Military Press Ltd
www.nmarchive.com
Published in association with The National Archives

Published by

The Naval & Military Press Ltd

Unit 10 Ridgewood Industrial Park,

Uckfield, East Sussex,

TN22 5QE England

Tel: +44 (0) 1825 749494

www.naval-military-press.com

www.nmarchive.com

This diary has been reprinted in facsimile from the original. Any imperfections are inevitably reproduced and the quality may fall short of modern type and cartographic standards.

© Crown Copyright
Images reproduced by permission of The National Archives, London, England, 2015.

Contents

Document type	Place/Title	Date From	Date To
Heading	WO95/1913/1 13 Royal Scots Regt Sep 1916		
Heading	13th-Battn., The Royal Scots.-Sept., 1916		
War Diary		01/09/1916	30/09/1916

WO95/1913-1

13 Royal Scots Regt

Sep 1916

SUBJECT.

13TH BATTN. The Royal Scots.

~~AUG~~ & SEPT, 1916

WAR DIARY or INTELLIGENCE SUMMARY

Army Form C 2118.

SEPTEMBER 1916

Date	Hour	Summary of Events and Information	Remarks
1		Battn in Brigade Reserve in FRICOURT ROAD lines. Situation quiet. The usual working parties were supplied. Running Road all day. Draft of 1. Other ranks + 2 and 2nd Lieuts D.S. Jones, R Kellar, J Ogden + G Smith joined the Battn. Casualties: 1 man killed.	
2		Brigade Reserve as above. Working parties supplied as usual. Weather improved. Casualties: 2nd R. Lusch wounded.	
3		Battn relieved 6th Cameron Hders in the Front line. Disposition of Coys:- "A" in INTERMEDIATE TRENCH, "B" in MILL STREET, "C" at CEMETERY + TOTLAND ALLEY (S. 9.d), "D" in O.G.I. Heavy shelling of the INTERMEDIATE LINE, otherwise situation fairly quiet. Casualties: 1 man killed 11 wounded.	
4		Battalion relieved by 1st Northumberland Fusiliers during the evening + moved to bivouacs E of ALBERT. (E.5.B). Relief reasonably at intervals. Draft of 58 other ranks joined the Battn.	
5		Moved at 7.50 AM to bivouacs NE of LAVIEVILLE, arriving there at 9.30.	

WAR DIARY or INTELLIGENCE SUMMARY

Army Form C 2118.

13th (S.) BN. ROYAL SCOTS

Instructions regarding War Diaries and Intelligence Summaries are contained in F.S. Regs., Part II and the Staff Manual respectively. Title Pages will be prepared in manuscript.

Place.	Date	Hour	Summary of Events and Information.	Remarks and references to Appendices
	6	A.M.	Weather stormy & ground very sodden.	
	7		The day spent in cleaning up lines, clothing & equipment & sundry inspections. Weather much better.	
	8		Parades & drill during the morning. Two companies bathed in stream near MERICOURT. Two Companies: football.	
	9		Parades &c. as for the 8th. Baths at HENENCOURT allotted & used by A & B Coys in the afternoon. Lt Col Jardine, 2/Lts 2. Bennett & G.Armyquard.	
	10		Parades &c. as for the 8th. C & D Companies bathed at HENENCOURT	
	11		Divine Service during the morning. Football in the afternoon. Battn practical attack at 6.30 a.m., involved of early morning harass. Packed Brigade attack in fields S. of LAVIEVILLE from 9.30 a.m. to 1.15 p.m. Companies using Leslie Disinfector during the afternoon. Draft of 32 other ranks joined the Battn. Weather good. Captain J. Little, Chaplain, returned to UK.	
	12		Heavy thunderstorm with exceptionally heavy rain at the great overnight fall made the going of his guns liquid Moved at 7.45 a.m. to bivouacs E of ALBERT (L.S.C.). 2nd Lieuts G.S. Hoar, D.B. Crombie, R. Laurie, J.J. Lumsdin & A. Brown joined the Battn.	
	13		Battalion left bivouacs at 7.45 a.m. & reached the 9th Black Watch in lines	

Army Form C 2118.

WAR DIARY
or
INTELLIGENCE SUMMARY
(Erase heading not required).

Instructions regarding War Diaries and Intelligence Summaries are contained in F.S. Regs., Part II and the Staff Manual respectively. Title Pages will be prepared in manuscript.

Place.	Date	Hour	Summary of Events and Information.	Remarks and references to Appendices
in the vicinity of SHELTER WOOD & FRICOURT ROAD. Carnoches N12.	14		Carrying parties, totalling 250 men, were supplied by the Battn during the day. Left lines at SHELTER WOOD at 9 p.m. Carnoches N12.	
	15		Battn relieved the 6/7th Royal Scots Fusiliers in the front line. Last Company ("B" Coy) reported in position at 4:40 A.M. "A" left, Advance. Guard, 1 June, "B" Coy on the right "D" Coy on the left. 2nd "C" Coy right "A" left. Usual bombardment of "Lennox" or MARTINPUICH and the trenches in front at dawn. At 6 A.M. "tanks" on right & left could be seen advancing. At 6.30 A.M bombardment became intense and the men went on. Luckily no hostile fire, enemy apparently taken by surprise. Battn suffered many casualties from own own artillery fire. At 7.5 A.M. Capt R.J.M. Climie (O.C.? Coy) came back wounded & reported objective gained. Posten consolidated & many prisoners sent back, including a Batalion Commander & his Adjutant. Some patrols went into MARTINPUICH about 9.20 a.m. and captured about 20 more prisoners.	

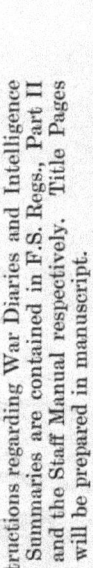

WAR DIARY
or
INTELLIGENCE SUMMARY

Army Form C 2118.

(Erase heading not required).

Place.	Date	Hour	Summary of Events and Information.	Remarks and references to Appendices
	16		6th Cameron Bttn. went through MARTINPUICH + occupied trench on N side. At 11 pm A + D Coys went up to support them + A Coy on the right gained touch with the 50th Division. Casualties: Wounded - Captains R.I. McChristie + M.C. Fish. Lieut L. McFarlane, 2nd Lt. P. Smith, W. Lowrie, J. Ogston, P. Gillatly, W.R. Laurie, G.B. Berry. N.C.O.s + men 23 killed, 143 wounded, 95 missing. A + D Coys returned to their original objective trench. MARTINPUICH heavily shelled by the enemy all day. 2nd Lt. R.F. Scott rejoined the Battn. Draft of 16 other ranks + 2nd Lt. A. Brown joined the Battn. Casualties:- 2nd Lt. J.L. Lowrie missing. N.C.O.s + men 8 killed + 14 wounded. Capt. D.E. McLean (Chaplain) joined Battn. for duty.	
	17		Battn. remained in the trench they had originally dug and continued to consolidate. Battn. relieved in the evening by 5th Seaforth + moved back to 6th AVENUE + KOYLI TRENCH. 2nd Lt. '6' Coy. W O.C.I. Casualties:- 2nd Lt. J.F.G. Turner + A. Brown wounded. Draft of 20 other ranks joined Battn.	

WAR DIARY or INTELLIGENCE SUMMARY

(Erase heading not required).

Army Form C 2118.

Instructions regarding War Diaries and Intelligence Summaries are contained in F.S. Regs., Part II and the Staff Manual respectively. Title Pages will be prepared in manuscript.

Place	Date	Hour	Summary of Events and Information.	Remarks and references to Appendices
	18		Batt. relieved by the 10th Northumberland Fusiliers at 3.30 p.m. Raining heavily. CONTALMAISON heavily shelled as 'A' Coy passed through. Batt. rested just E. of ALBERT & had tea. Marched on to MÉAULTE. Batt. in billets at 8 p.m. Casualties:- 1 new wounded.	
	19		Marched out at 11.5 a.m. to BAZIEUX WOOD passing through LAVIÉVILLE & BRÉSLE. Batt. had dinners outside the wood. Advanced in the wood. Raining heavily & ground very foul.	
	20		Companies cleaning up & reorganising. 2nd Lt. A.C. Farquharson & 60 other ranks joined for duty.	
	21		Companies bathing, drilling & reorganising. Weather improved. Batter.	
	22		C. & D. Coys bathing. Brigadier General inspected Battalion.	
	23		at Company drill. Draft of 21 other ranks joined Batt. Weather improved. Commanding Officer inspected the Batt. during the morning. Isolence competition in the afternoon.	
	24		Divine Service in the morning. Sports & company route marches during the afternoon. Weather fair.	

Army Form C. 2118.

WAR DIARY or INTELLIGENCE SUMMARY.
(Erase heading not required.)

Place	Date	Hour	Summary of Events and Information	Remarks and references to Appendices
	25		Battn. inspected by the G.O.C. 45th Infantry Brigade. Battn. moved to billets in BAZIEUX in the afternoon. Draft of 25 O.Rs joined. Joined the Battn. Weather good.	
	26		(a) Company instructing strong points under instructions of 2nd Lt Haggie & Eaton Bros. Battn. at musketry on Brigade range.	
	27		2 Company instructing strong points 16 other ranks of each A + D Coys. instruction in rapid loading. Tattoo on Tactical Exercises in the afternoon. Weather unsettled.	
	28		Battn. route march in the morning, with Advance & Rearguard. Practised attack on return journey. Bombing during the afternoon. Lecture by Army Instructor of Physical Training & Bayonet fighting to all Officers & NCOs. Draft of 19 O.Rs joined for duty.	
	29		Raining heavily. Kit inspections. Lecture by Company Officers + Bayonet fighting.	
	30		Companies under their R.S.M. for drill afternoon. Lt Cameron Ebro Jones, 2nd Lts W.D. Howat, J.A. Fenwick, A. Morton joined Battn.